The State Funeral of Sir Winston Churchill

30th January, 1965

This edition published in 2013 by
Unicorn Press Ltd
66 Charlotte Street
London W1T 4QE

www.unicornpress.org

First published in 1965 by George Rainbird Limited

ISBN 978 1 9065 09354

1 3 5 7 9 10 8 6 4 2

Cover design by Camilla Fellas
Repro by XY Digital, London
Printed in China for Latitude Press Ltd

The State Funeral of Sir Winston Churchill

30th January, 1965

A Sketchbook by

Charles Mozley

With a Foreword by

The Rt. Hon. Nicholas Soames, MP

With the Tribute by

The Rt. Hon. Sir Robert Menzies

KT, PC, CH, QC

Former Prime Minister of Australia

Unicorn Press Ltd

London

Foreword for the New Edition of *The State Funeral of Sir Winston Churchill* by The Rt. Hon. Nicholas Soames, MP

It is a great pleasure to be invited to write a short foreword for the republication of this book which vividly brings to life the State Funeral of Sir Winston Churchill on that bitter January day in 1965. These remarkable pictures by Charles Mozley are truly evocative of an event in our Nation's history, which for anyone who took part or was there, will never be forgotten.

Looking back on it, having marched in the procession with my father and brother and other family mourners, the abiding memory is that there was not a false note struck all day, as the Nation paid its tribute to my grandfather, in a most moving way.

As my grandmother, Clementine Churchill, said to my mother at the end of the day, 'You know, Mary, it wasn't a funeral - it was a Triumph.'

And indeed it was and it is beautifully captured in this book.

The Rt. Hon. Nicholas Soames, MP
July, 2013

The Tribute, delivered by Sir Robert Menzies, Former Prime Minister of Australia, on the Occasion of Sir Winston Churchill's Funeral, Saturday 30th January, 1965

As this historic procession goes through the streets of London to the Tower Pier, I have the honour of speaking to you from the crypt of St Paul's Cathedral.

I do this in two capacities. One is that I, Prime Minister of Australia, happen to be, in point of time, the Senior Commonwealth Prime Minister, and therefore speak on behalf of a remarkable world organisation which owes more than it can ever express to our departed leader, Sir Winston Churchill. He is one of the famous men whom we thank and praise.

My second capacity is more personal and more intimate. I am sure that you, most of you, have thought about Sir Winston Churchill a great deal, and with warmth in your hearts and in your recollections. Some day, some year, there will be old men and women whose pride it will be to say – 'I lived in Churchill's time.' Some will be able to say – 'I saw him, and I heard him – the unforgettable voice and the immortal words.' And some will be able to say – 'I knew him, and talked with him, and was his friend.'

This I can, with a mixture of pride and humility, say for myself. The memory of this moves me deeply now that he is dead, but is gloriously remembered by me as he goes to his burial amid the sorrow, and pride, and thanks, of all of you who stand and feel for yourselves and for so many millions.

Many of you will not need to be reminded, but some, the younger among you, the inheritors of his master-strokes for freedom, may be glad to be told that your country, and mine, and all the free countries of the world, stood at the very gates of destiny, in 1940 and 1941, when the Nazi tyranny threatened to engulf us, and when there was no 'second front' except our own. This was the great crucial moment of modern history. What was at stake was not some theory of government but the whole and personal freedom of men, and women, and children. And the battle for them was a battle against great odds. That battle had to be won not only in the air and on the sea and in the field, but in the hearts and minds of ordinary people with a deep capacity for heroism. It was then that Winston Churchill was called, by Almighty God, as our faith makes us believe, to stand as our leader and our inspirer.

There were, in 1940, defeatists, who felt that prudence required submission or such terms as might be had. There were others who, while not accepting the inevitability of defeat, thought that victory was impossible.

Winston Churchill scorned to fall into either category, and he was right. With courage, and matchless eloquence, and human understanding, he inspired us and led us to victory.

In the whole of recorded modern history, this was, I believe, the one occasion when one man, with soaring imagination, with one fire burning in him, and with one unrivalled capacity for conveying it to others, won a crucial victory not only for the forces (for there were many heroes in those days) but for the very spirit of human freedom.

And so, on this great day, we thank him, and we thank God for him.

There are two other things I want to say to you, on a day which neither you nor I will ever willingly forget.

One is that Winston Churchill was not an institution but a man; a man of wit and chuckling humour, and penetrating understanding, not a man who spoke to us from the mountain tops, but one who expressed the simple and enduring feelings of ordinary men and women. It was because he was a great Englishman that he was able to speak for the English people. It was because he was a great Commonwealth statesman that he was able to warm hearts and inspire courage right around the seven seas. It was because he was a great human being that, in our darkest days, he lit the lamps of hope at many firesides and released so many from the chains of despair.

There has been nobody like him in our lifetimes. We must, and do, thank God for him, and strive to be worthy of his example.

And the second thing I will never forget is this. Winston Churchill's wife is with us here in London; a great and gracious lady in her own right. Could I today send her your love, and mine? She has suffered an irreparable personal loss. But she has proud and enduring memories. Happy memories, I venture to say. We share her sorrow, but I know that she would wish us to share with her those rich remembrances which the thought of the great man evokes.

There have been, in the course of recorded history, some men of power who have cast shadows across the world. Winston Churchill, on the contrary, was a fountain of light and of hope.

As I end my talk to you from the crypt of St Paul's, with its reminders of Nelson and Wellington, those marvellous defenders of long ago, the body of Winston Churchill goes in procession through the streets of London; his London, our London, this most historic city, this ancient home of freedom, this place through which, in the very devastation and fire of war, his voice rang with courage, and defiance, and hope, and rugged confidence.

His body will be carried on the Thames, a river full of history. With one heart we all feel, with one mind we all acknowledge, that it will never have borne a more precious burden, or been enriched by more splendid memories.

The Rt. Hon. Sir Robert Menzies KT, PC, CH, QC
January, 1965

LIST OF SKETCHES

19